ALL ABOUT
BUGS & SPIDERS

by Dee Phillips

ALL ABOUT
BUGS & SPIDERS

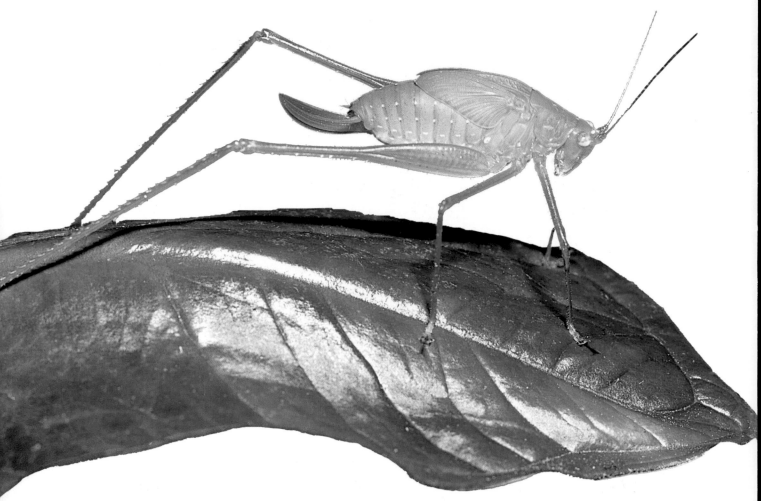

Copyright © **ticktock Entertainment Ltd 2006**

First published in Great Britain in 2006 by **ticktock Ltd.,**

Unit 2, Orchard Business Centre, North Farm Road, Tunbridge Wells, Kent, TN2 3XF

ISBN 1 86007 863 X pbk

Printed in China

CONTENTS

Words that appear in **bold** are explained in the glossary.

HIDDEN WORLDS

Bugs, spiders, and other creepy crawlies can be found all over the world. They live on land, in water, and underground. Some make their homes under rocks, others on trees or in rotting leaves, and some even live in our own houses.

There are more insects around than you might think. Many are small and stay hidden under rocks or in small cracks. Keep your eyes open and see how many you can find.

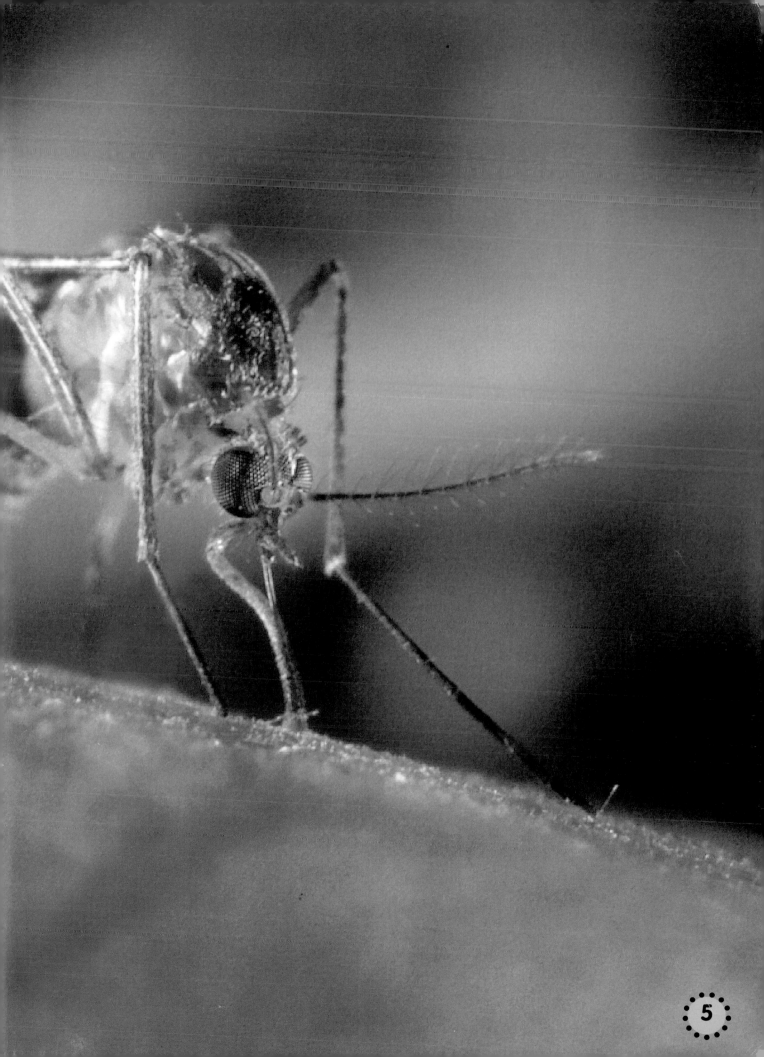

MEET THE BUGS & SPIDERS

Most of the creatures we call bugs are insects. This means they have six legs and a body divided into three parts—the **head**, the **thorax**, and the **abdomen**. Spiders, centipedes, millipedes, slugs, snails, and leeches are not insects because they do not have this body shape.

Insects have an interesting life cycle. Some insects are called **nymphs** when they hatch from the egg. As they grow bigger they gradually grow more and more like the adult insect. Other insects are called **larvae** when they hatch from the egg. When they reach their full size they make a shell called a **pupa** or cocoon around themselves. Inside the pupa they change to the adult insect. Young nymphs and larvae look very different from adult insects.

Some bugs and spiders can be brightly colored, like butterflies, or dull, like ants. Some have wings, but not all can fly. See how many insects you know.

ANTS

Ants can live almost anywhere. There are thousands of different kinds. Some ants eat tiny insects. Others feed on **nectar** and **honeydew**. Ants feel around with two pointy **antennae.**

Some ants eat small insects like caterpillars. Some ants farm aphids. The aphids give the ants honeydew in return for the ants' protection.

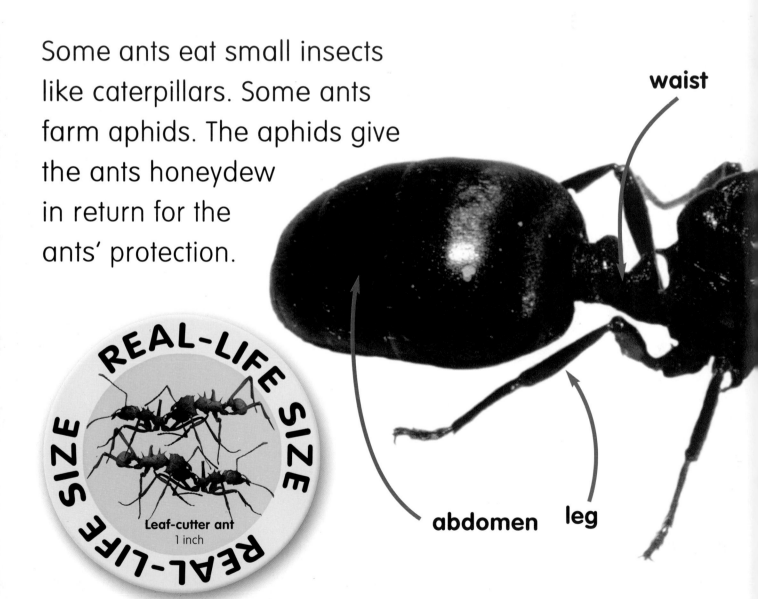

waist

abdomen leg

REAL-LIFE SIZE
REAL-LIFE SIZE

Leaf-cutter ant
1 inch

Ants live in a group called a **colony.** One or more queen ants lay all the eggs. Female workers raise the young and find food. Only queens and males have wings.

head

antenna

thorax

The queen ant lays an egg.

A **larva** hatches from an egg.

When full grown, the larva changes into a **pupa**.

An ant hatches from the pupa.

9

APHIDS

Aphids are small, soft-bodied insects that live on plants and trees. They feed on **sap** from young leaves. There are many different kinds of aphids.

Aphids produce a sugary waste called **honeydew**. This sweet liquid is a tasty food for ants, bees, and wasps.

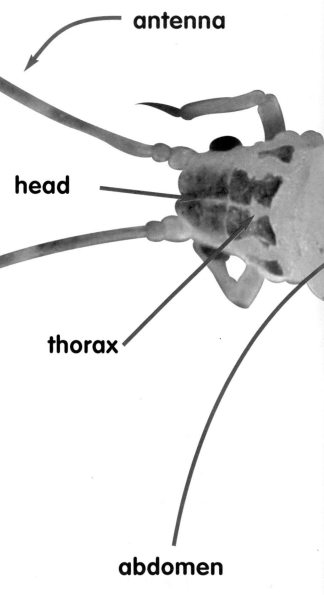

antenna

head

thorax

abdomen

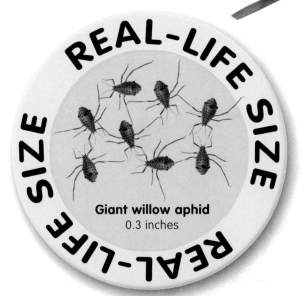

REAL-LIFE SIZE
REAL-LIFE SIZE

Giant willow aphid
0.3 inches

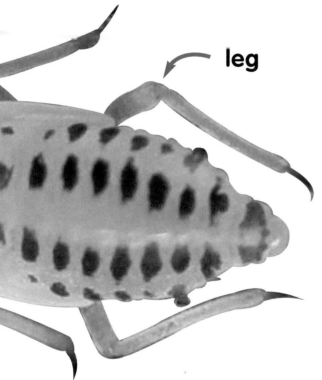

leg

Aphids reproduce very quickly. During the summer they produce wingless females. In the fall they produce winged males and females that fly away to new places.

Aphid Life Cycle

A female aphid lays an egg.

A wingless female **nymph** hatches from the egg.

The wingless female lays more eggs which hatch into wingless females.

In the fall, wingless females lay eggs which hatch into winged male and female aphids.

11

ARMY ANTS

Army ants live in groups in tropical forests. They move from place to place, making a nest with their own bodies each time they stop.

Army ants usually eat small insects such as grasshoppers and caterpillars. But sometimes they attack in big groups. Then they can catch larger **prey** like snakes, chickens, and even goats!

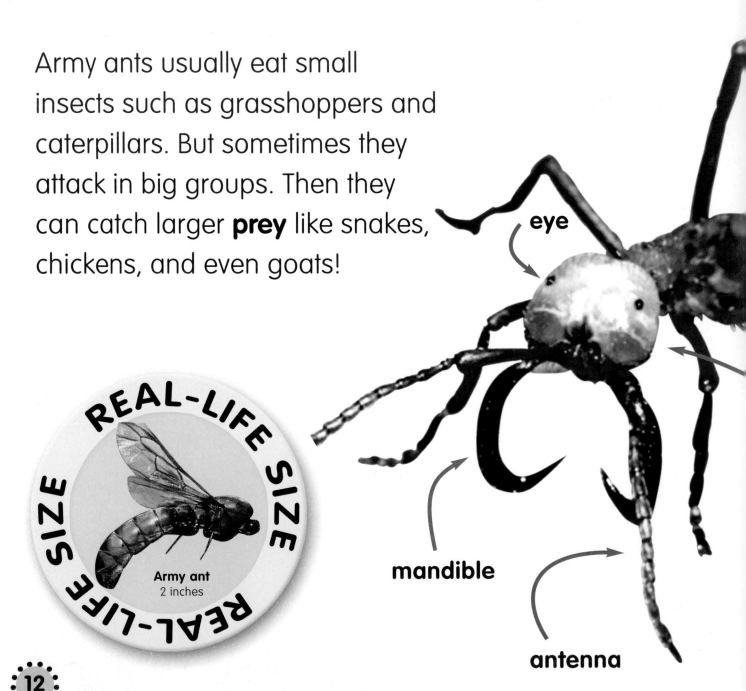

eye

mandible

antenna

REAL-LIFE SIZE
REAL-LIFE SIZE

Army ant
2 inches

Army ants have tiny eyes but cannot actually see. They use their **antennae** to feel their way around.

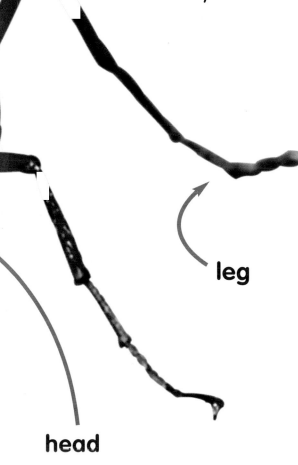

leg

head

Army Ant Life Cycle

The queen ant lays an egg.

A **larva** hatches from the egg.

When full grown, the larva becomes a **pupa**.

An ant hatches from the pupa.

BEDBUGS

Bedbugs are small, flat insects. They get their name because they live in beds! They also live in cracks in floors and walls. Bedbugs are parasites that bite humans and feed on their blood.

A bedbug bite looks like a line of tiny bumps on the victim's skin.

thorax

beak

head

REAL-LIFE SIZE

Common bedbug
0.25 inches

The brown bedbug turns red when it drinks blood.

Bedbugs hide during the day and come out at night to look for food.

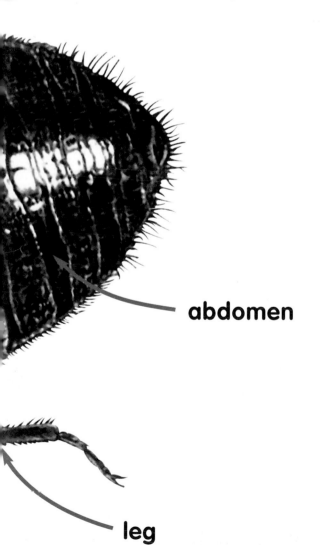

abdomen

leg

Bedbug Life Cycle

The female bedbug lays eggs.

A **nymph** hatches out of an egg.

The nymph gets bigger and bigger.

The nymph becomes an adult bedbug.

BUTTERFLIES

Butterflies are winged insects. They have a mouth shaped like a straw. They need this special mouth for sucking **nectar** from flowers.

There are thousands of different kinds of butterflies. They have two pairs of colorful wings.

antennae

abdomen

hind wing

How **BIG** is a **butterfly?**

12 inches

0.6 inches

Smallest:
Western pygmy blue

Largest:
Queen Alexandra's birdwing

forewing

The wings of the leaf butterfly below look just like real leaves! The way it blends into its surroundings is called **camouflage.**

Butterfly Life Cycle

A female butterfly lays an egg.

A **larva** called a caterpillar hatches from the egg.

When full grown, the larva turns into a **pupa** or chrysalis.

A butterfly hatches from the chrysalis.

CATERPILLARS

Caterpillars are the **larvae** of butterflies and moths. They live in many different places—in trees, underground, in plant stems, and even inside leaves.

Most caterpillars eat leaves and flowers. Some eat wood, and others eat roots. Caterpillars spend most of their time eating!

sucker legs

How **BIG** is a **caterpillar?**

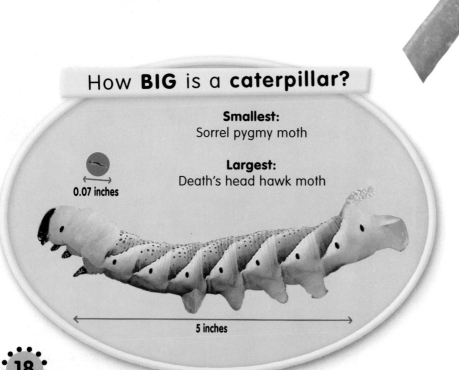

Smallest:
Sorrel pygmy moth

0.07 inches

Largest:
Death's head hawk moth

5 inches

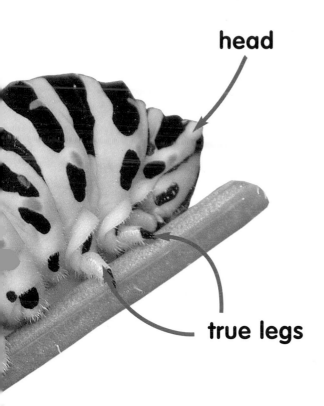

head

true legs

Caterpillars are eating machines. When a lot of caterpillars are eating together, you can actually hear munching noises!

Caterpillar Life Cycle

The female butterfly or moth lays an egg.

A caterpillar hatches from the egg.

When full grown, the **larva** changes into a **pupa** or chrysalis.

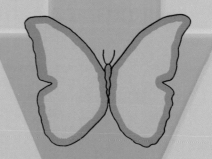

A butterfly or moth hatches from the pupa.

CENTIPEDES

Centipedes are fast-moving creatures with lots of legs. They eat insects, worms, spiders, slugs, and other small animals. They use poison to kill their **prey.** Some live for six years.

The name centipede means "100 legs," but no centipede has exactly 100. Most have about 30 legs. But one kind has 254!

antenna

head

How **BIG** is a **centipede?**

0.4 inches

Smallest:
Hoffman's dwarf centipede

12 inches

Largest:
Giant Peruvian centipede

a body made up of many parts, called segments

Centipedes like to live in damp places under rocks and logs, or under piles of fallen leaves.

one pair of legs on each segment

Centipede Life Cycle

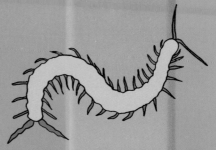

The female centipede lays an egg.

A **nymph** hatches from the egg.

The nymph grows up to be an adult centipede.

CICADAS

Cicadas are large flying insects. Their **compound eyes** help them see in many directions at once. Cicadas use their sharp beak to suck **sap** from plants.

Male cicadas are noisy! In the summer, they sing a screechy song to attract a mate. They make the sound by moving small parts on their **abdomen**.

three legs on each side

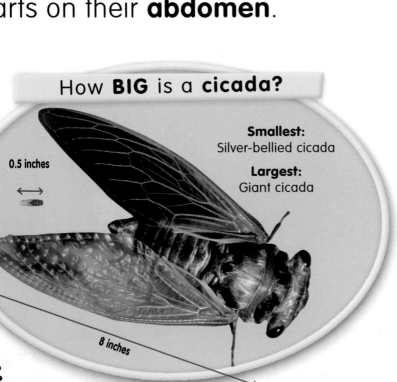

How **BIG** is a **cicada**?

0.5 inches

Smallest: Silver-bellied cicada

Largest: Giant cicada

8 inches

two pairs of wings

compound eyes

The female cicada lays an egg in the stem of a plant.

A **nymph** hatches from the egg and falls to the ground.

Some species take 17 years to become adults. All of the cicadas in one place may become adults on the same day.

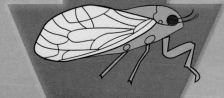

When full grown the nymph becomes a cicada.

COCKROACHES

Cockroaches are insects. Most live outside in the wild. But some live in places where food is stored or prepared. Cockroaches eat almost anything, even paper and soap!

Cockroaches can run fast. They hide in dark places during the day and come out to look for food at night.

abdomen

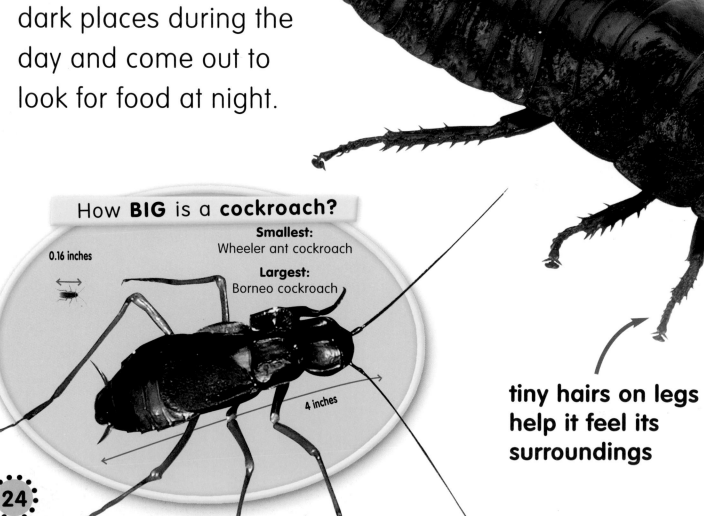

How **BIG** is a **cockroach?**

Smallest:
Wheeler ant cockroach

0.16 inches

Largest:
Borneo cockroach

4 inches

tiny hairs on legs help it feel its surroundings

A cockroach has two body parts called **cerci** at the end of its abdomen. The cerci are used to sense when danger is near.

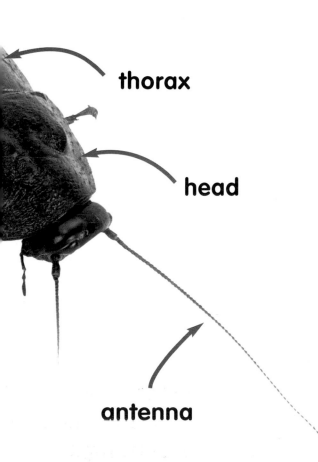

thorax

head

antenna

Cockroach Life Cycle

A female cockroach lays an egg.

A **nymph** hatches from the egg.

The nymph becomes an adult cockroach.

DRAGONFLIES

Dragonflies are insects with beautiful, **transparent** wings. There are about 5,000 different kinds. They are all strong fliers that can stop and **hover** in one place.

A dragonfly **nymph** lives underwater. An adult lives on land (and in the air!), near water.

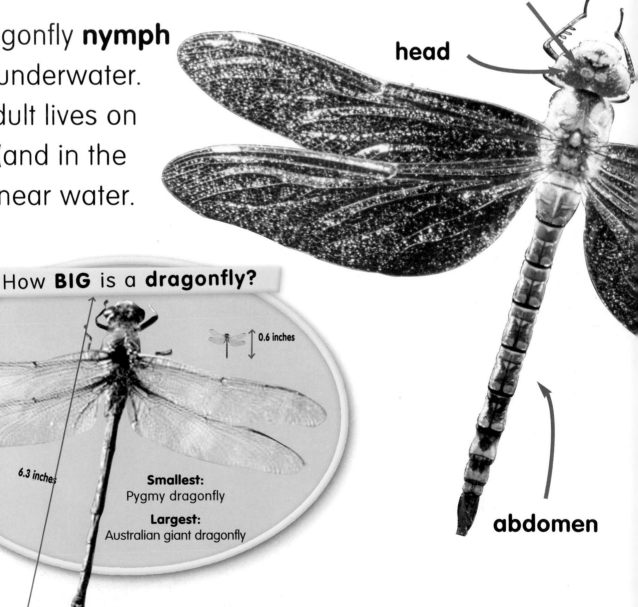

large eyes

head

abdomen

How **BIG** is a **dragonfly?**

0.6 inches

6.3 inches

Smallest:
Pygmy dragonfly

Largest:
Australian giant dragonfly

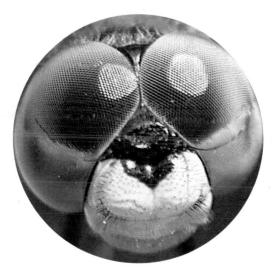

A dragonfly's large **compound eyes** cover most of its **head**. They help it catch its dinner: other flying insects!

forewing

hind wing

Dragonfly Life Cycle

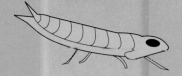

A female dragonfly lays an egg in or near water.

A **nymph** hatches from the egg and lives underwater.

The full grown nymph crawls out of the water and becomes a dragonfly.

DUNG BEETLES

There are many different kinds of dung beetles. They eat the dung, or poo, of other animals! These helpful beetles keep our Earth clean, and the soil healthy.

Some dung beetles are very strong. They can roll a ball of dung 50 times their own weight.

hard wing cases

six hairy legs

How **BIG** is a **dung beetle?**

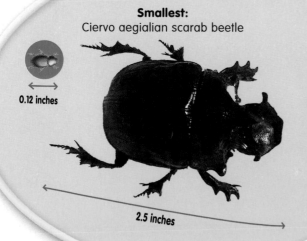

Smallest:
Ciervo aegialian scarab beetle

0.12 inches

Largest:
Elephant dung beetle

2.5 inches

Some female dung beetles lay their eggs in a ball of dung. When the **larvae** hatch, they have food waiting for them!

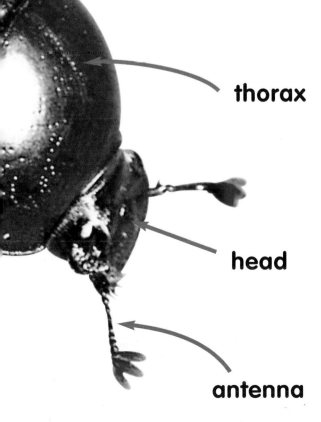

thorax

head

antenna

Dung Beetle Life Cycle

A female dung beetle lays an egg in dung.

A **larva** hatches from the egg.

When full grown, the larva turns into a **pupa**.

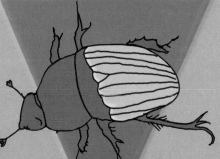

A dung beetle hatches from the pupa.

EARWIGS

Earwigs are often found in gardens. They live under stones and on plants. They mostly come out at night. The males have longer, more curved **forceps** than the females.

The earwig got its name because people used to believe that it crawled into their ears when they were asleep. But they don't really do that.

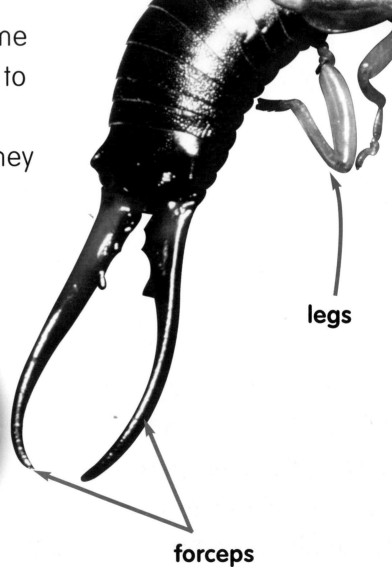

legs

forceps

REAL-LIFE SIZE

Saint Helena giant earwig

3 inches

REAL-LIFE SIZE

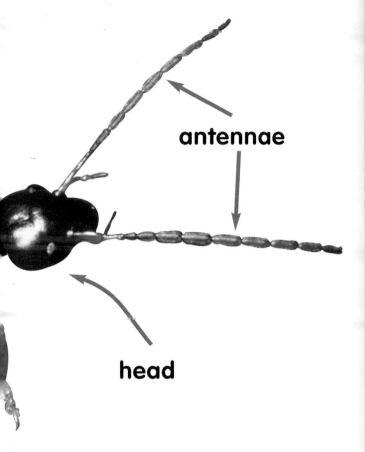

antennae

head

Female earwigs are good mothers. They look after their eggs and keep them clean by licking them. They feed the young earwigs when they hatch.

Earwig Life Cycle

The female earwig lays an egg.

A **nymph** hatches out of the egg.

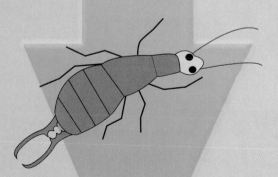

The nymph becomes an adult earwig.

FIREFLIES

Fireflies are also called lightning bugs. They are winged beetles. Most kinds of fireflies can make the end of their **abdomen** light up. They flash this light at night, to attract a mate.

Fireflies eat other insects, slugs, and snails. Sometimes they even eat other fireflies.

leg

pronotum
(protective plate)

the head is
under here

antennae

REAL-LIFE SIZE
REAL-LIFE SIZE

Pyralis firefly
1.2 inches

wing case

Like many beetles, the firefly has hard **wing cases** that close over its thin wings when the insect is not flying.

Firefly Life Cycle

The female firefly lays an egg.

A **larva** hatches from the egg.

When full grown, the larva becomes a **pupa**.

A firefly hatches from the pupa.

FLEAS

Fleas are a type of insect called **parasites**. They live on the bodies of people or animals and feed on their blood.

Each kind of flea lives on a different kind of **host,** such as cats or dogs. Fleas use their sharp mouthparts to push through skin.

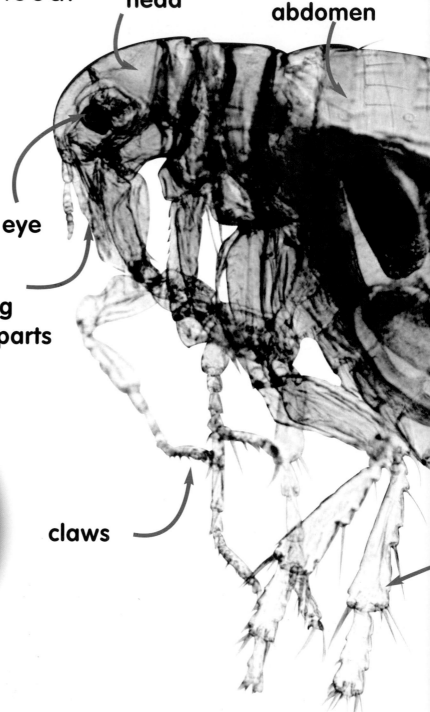

head

abdomen

eye

piercing mouthparts

claws

REAL-LIFE SIZE

Mountain beaver flea
0.3 inches

A tiny flea has powerful back legs. It can can leap as far as 6 inches to land on a host animal.

long back legs

Flea Life Cycle

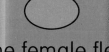

The female flea lays an egg.

A **larva** hatches out of the egg.

When full grown, the larva turns into a **pupa**.

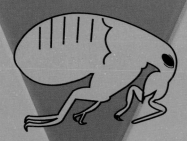

A flea hatches out of the pupa.

FLIES

Flies are very good at . . . flying! They can beat their wings 200 times a second. Many flies use their **saliva** to turn fruit and other plant material into liquid food. Other flies eat insects or drink blood.

Flies have tiny hooks and sticky pads on their feet to grip the places they land. They can even hang upside down!

abdomen

wings

leg

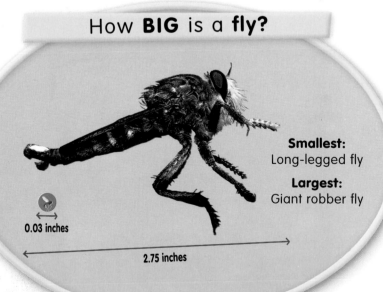

How **BIG** is a **fly?**

Smallest:
Long-legged fly

Largest:
Giant robber fly

0.03 inches

2.75 inches

Flies taste their food with hairs on their feet.

Fly Life Cycle

The female fly lays an egg.

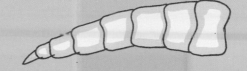

A **larva** or maggot hatches from the egg.

When full grown, the larva turns into a **pupa**.

A fly hatches out of the pupa.

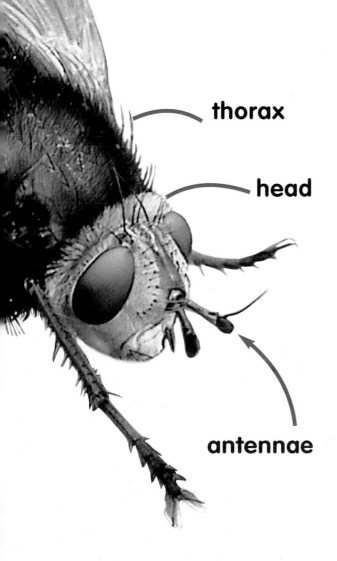

thorax

head

antennae

GIANT MILLIPEDES

Millipede means "thousand legs", but no millipede really has that many! Some have up to 750 legs, but others have as few as 24. Millipedes cannot see very well. They mainly come out at night.

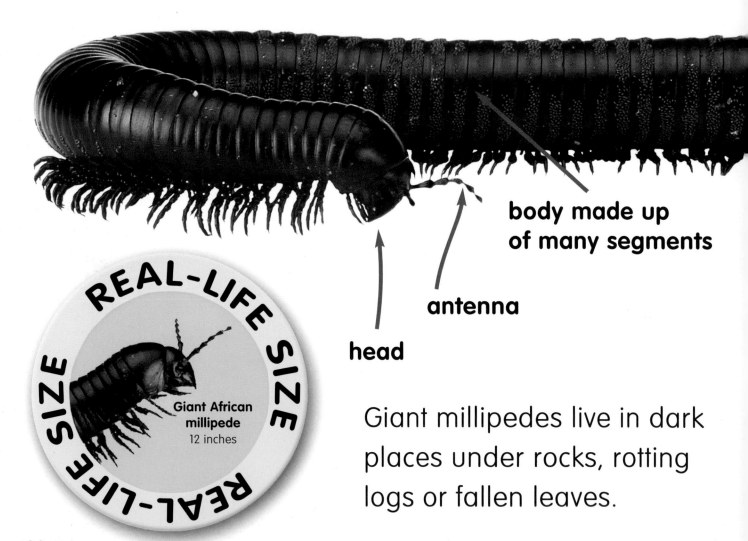

body made up of many segments

antenna

head

REAL-LIFE SIZE
REAL-LIFE SIZE

Giant African millipede
12 inches

Giant millipedes live in dark places under rocks, rotting logs or fallen leaves.

If a millipede senses danger, it curls up so that its **head** and soft underside are protected.

two pairs of legs on each body segment

The female millipede lays an egg.

A young millipede hatches from the egg – as it gets older, more legs and segments grow.

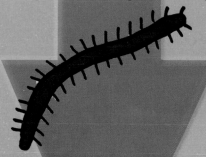

The young millipede grows up to be an adult.

GRASSHOPPERS

Grasshoppers are a group of insects that are very good jumpers. They eat grasses and other plants.

Male grasshoppers rub their back legs against their leathery wings to make a loud, chirping sound. This sound attracts female grasshoppers.

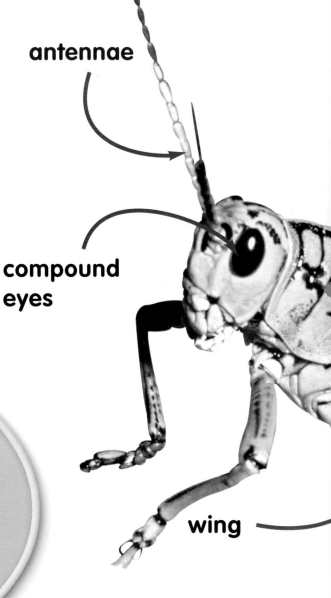

antennae

compound eyes

wing

How **BIG** is a **grasshopper?**

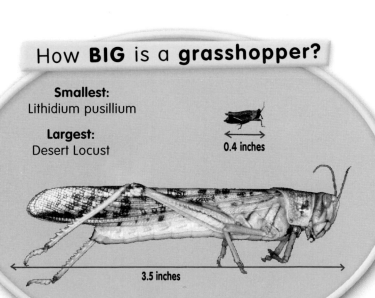

Smallest:
Lithidium pusillium

Largest:
Desert Locust

0.4 inches

3.5 inches

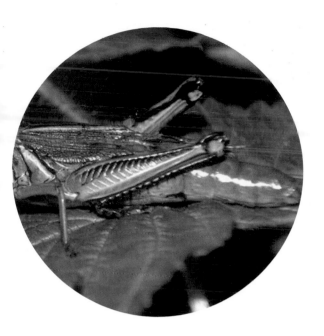

To escape danger, a grasshopper may jump rather than fly away. It has strong back legs.

strong back legs

Grasshopper Life Cycle

The female grasshopper lays an egg.

A **nymph** hatches from the egg.

The nymph grows into an adult grasshopper.

GROUND BEETLES

Not all ground beetles live on the ground. Some live under the bark of trees. They hide in tiny cracks during the day and come out at night to eat. Ground beetles have long legs and can run very fast.

Most ground beetles are **predators**. They eat small insects, worms, and slugs. A few just eat seeds. They use their strong jaws to bite their food.

jaws

antennae

head

How **BIG** is a **ground beetle?**

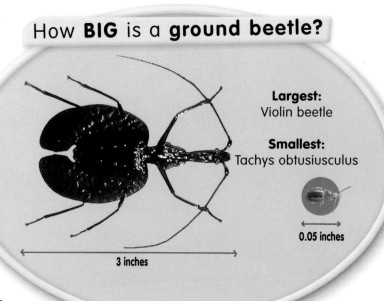

Largest:
Violin beetle

Smallest:
Tachys obtusiusculus

0.05 inches

3 inches

Some ground beetles are brightly colored. They have shiny **wing cases** that gleam like jewels.

wing cases

leg

Ground Beetle Life Cycle

The female ground beetle lays an egg.

A **larva** hatches from the egg.

When full grown, the larva turns into a **pupa**.

A ground beetle comes out of the pupa.

HEAD LICE

Head lice are small wingless **parasites** that feed on human blood. They like living in clean hair.

Head lice have flat bodies. Their front legs have hooklike claws to grab on to the hairs on a person's head and neck.

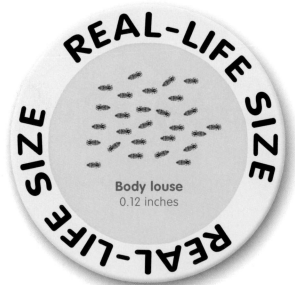

REAL-LIFE SIZE
REAL-LIFE SIZE

Body louse
0.12 inches

abdomen

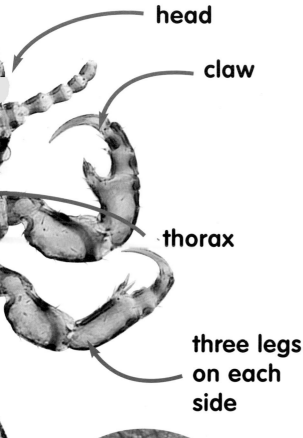

head

claw

thorax

three legs on each side

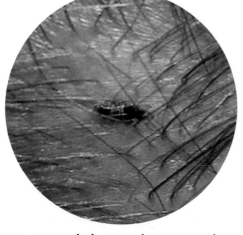

Head lice love clean human hair. They spread by crawling from head to head!

Head Louse Life Cycle

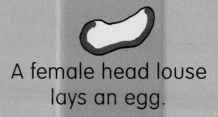

A female head louse lays an egg.

A **nymph** hatches from the egg.

The nymph becomes an adult head louse.

HONEYBEES

Honeybees live in large **colonies**. Each colony has a queen who lays the eggs. Male bees, called drones, mate with the queen, and the worker bees. Workers are female. They look after the **larvae**, make honey, and guard the nest.

Honeybees do a "waggle dance" to tell each other where the best flowers are.

two pairs
of wings

abdomen

baskets on the back legs
for carrying pollen

REAL-LIFE SIZE
REAL-LIFE SIZE

Giant honeybee
0.75 inches

compound eye

thorax

Honeybees feed on **nectar** and **pollen** collected from flowers.

Honeybee Life Cycle

The queen bee lays an egg.

A **larva** hatches from the egg.

The larva turns into a **pupa**.

A honeybee hatches from the pupa.

JUMPING SPIDERS

Jumping spiders are very small, but they can jump a long way. They have four pairs of eyes and can see **prey** up to 12 inches away. They are easily identified by their black and white markings.

Jumping spiders eat small insects. They do not make webs, since they catch prey by jumping on it.

abdomen

legs

REAL-LIFE SIZE REAL-LIFE SIZE REAL-LIFE SIZE

Green jumping spider
0.5 inches

A jumping spider can jump a long way for such a small spider. It leaps onto its prey before the insect can see it coming.

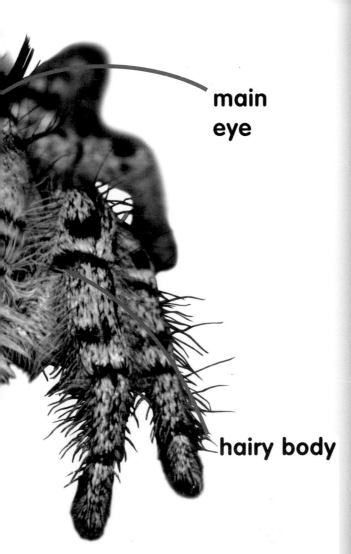

main eye

hairy body

Jumping Spider Life Cycle

A jumping spider lays an egg.

A spiderling hatches from the egg.

The spiderling grows up to be an adult.

LADYBUGS

Ladybugs are a kind of beetle. They help protect gardens by eating tiny pests called aphids.

Ladybugs have hard **wing cases** to protect their wings. The bright color tells birds, "I taste bad. Don't eat me!"

REAL-LIFE SIZE

Seven spot ladybird
0.25 inches

wings fold up when not in use

hard wing case

leg

antenna

head

During the winter, ladybugs **hibernate** under logs, leaves, or bark. They huddle together in big groups.

Ladybug Life Cycle

A female ladybug lays an egg.

A **larva** hatches from the egg.

When full grown, the larva becomes a **pupa**.

A ladybug hatches from the pupa.

LEAFHOPPERS

Leafhoppers are small insects that live on trees and plants. They make holes in the leaves of plants with their mouths and suck out the **sap**.

The mouth of a leafhopper is shaped like a straw.

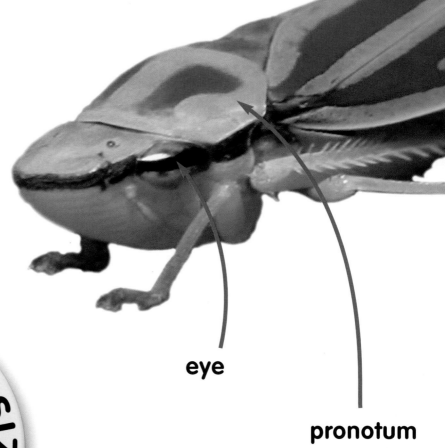

eye

pronotum (protective plate)

REAL-LIFE SIZE
REAL-LIFE SIZE

Ledromorpha planirostris
1 inch

forewings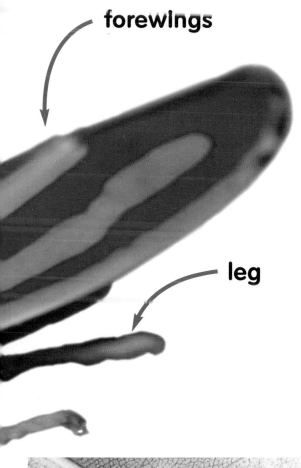

leg

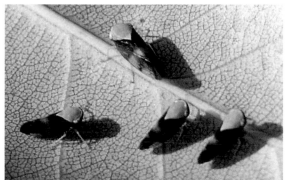

Leafhoppers make sounds to send messages to other leafhoppers. Humans cannot hear these sounds.

Leafhopper Life Cycle

The female leafhopper lays an egg.

A **nymph** hatches out of the egg.

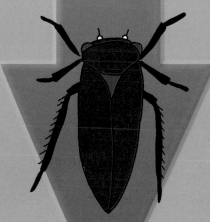

The nymph grows into an adult leafhopper.

LEECHES

Leeches are a type of worm. They live in water and on damp forest floors. Leeches have **suckers** at each end of their body. They use these to attach themselves to their **host** and to move along.

A leech's body is made of up of many segments, or sections. It has a small mouth at one end. Some kinds have two eyes. Others have as many as ten!

sucker

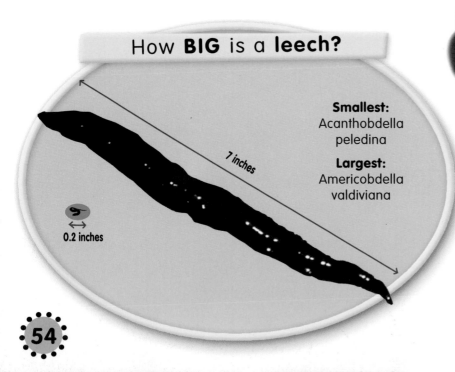

How **BIG** is a leech?

7 inches

0.2 inches

Smallest:
Acanthobdella
peledina

Largest:
Americobdella
valdiviana

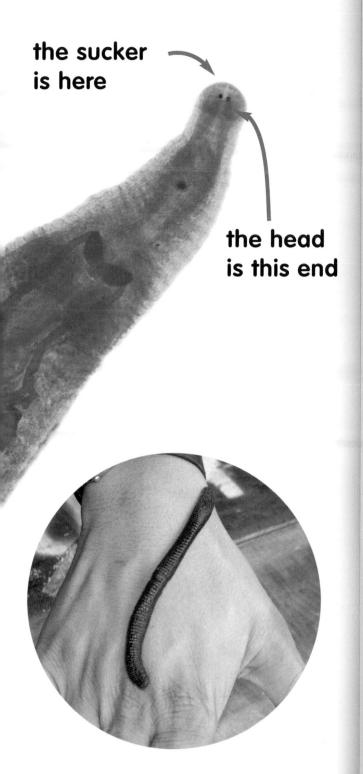

the sucker is here

the head is this end

A leech has a sucker at each end of its body. These suckers help it move and hold on while it eats.

Leech Life Cycle

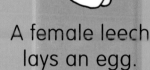

A female leech lays an egg.

The egg hatches into a young leech.

The young leech grows into an adult.

LOCUSTS

Young locusts are called hoppers and cannot fly. The adults are a large type of flying grasshopper. Locusts have very strong leg muscles, which help them spring into the air when they get ready to fly.

Locusts have very strong back legs. They can jump up to ten times their own length. They also have long wings for flying.

antenna

head

short front legs

strong back legs for jumping

REAL-LIFE SIZE
REAL-LIFE SIZE

Desert Locust
3.5 inches

Locusts travel together in a huge group called a swarm. They can gobble up an entire farm field very quickly.

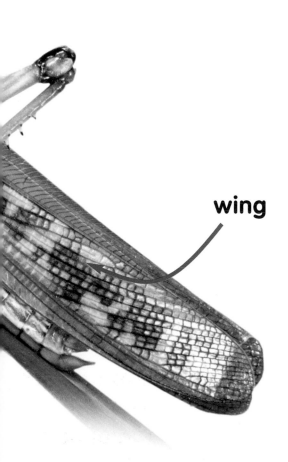

wing

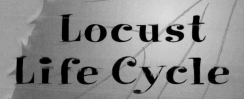

Locust Life Cycle

The female locust lays an egg, underground.

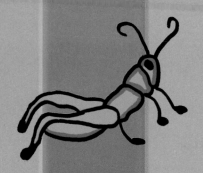

A **nymph** hatches from the egg.

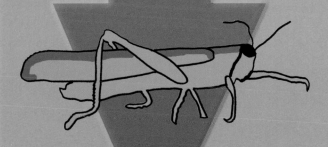

The nymph grows into an adult locust.

LONGHORN BEETLES

Longhorn beetles are a group of insects that are known for their long **antennae**. Their **larvae** eat wood and can damage trees.

leg

A longhorn beetle's antennae are often longer than its body!

wing cases

How **BIG** is a **longhorn beetle?**

Largest:
Giant longhorn beetle

3.5 inches

Smallest:
Long-horned beetle
(no special name)

0.2 inches

Some longhorn beetles have wasp-like markings to scare off **predators**.

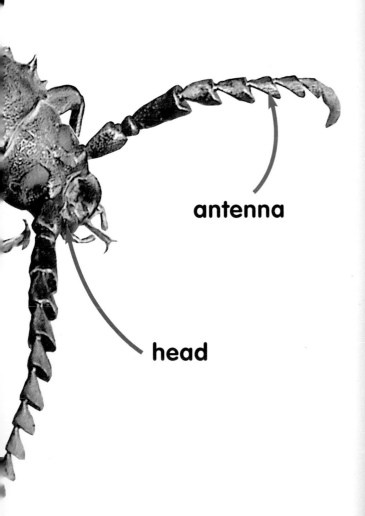

antenna

head

Longhorn Beetle Life Cycle

The female beetle lays an egg.

A **larva** hatches out of the egg.

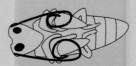

When full grown, the larva turns into a **pupa**.

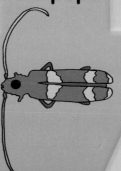

A beetle hatches from the pupa.

MOLE CRICKETS

Mole crickets live in underground **burrows**. They use their strong front legs for digging. Some kinds eat only roots and plants. Others also eat worms and **larvae**.

Male mole crickets make a chirping sound by rubbing their wings together.

head

large eyes

broad front legs

REAL-LIFE SIZE
REAL-LIFE SIZE

Prairie mole cricket
2 inches

longer back legs

Female mole crickets stay in their burrows to protect their **nymphs**.

Mole Cricket Life Cycle

The female mole cricket lays an egg.

A **nymph** hatches out of the egg.

The nymph grows into an adult mole cricket.

61

MOSQUITOES

Mosquitoes are flies. There are about 3,000 different kinds. The females drink animal blood. The males drink **nectar**.

Some mosquitoes can spread a deadly disease called malaria. Many people around the world die of malaria each year.

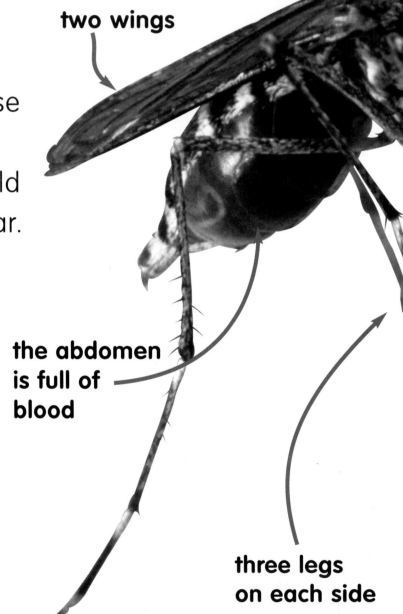

two wings

the abdomen is full of blood

three legs on each side

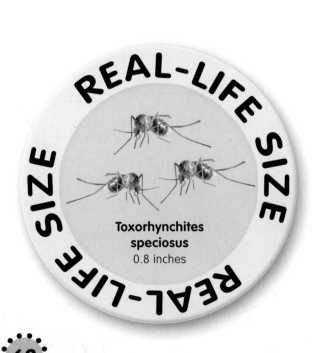

REAL-LIFE SIZE
REAL-LIFE SIZE

Toxorhynchites speciosus
0.8 inches

antenna

mouth

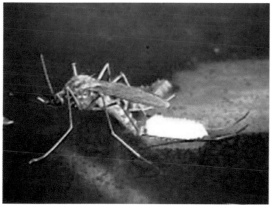

Female mosquitoes lay their eggs on the surface of water.

Mosquito Life Cycle

The female lays an egg.

A **larva** hatches out of the egg and lives underwater.

When full grown, the larva changes into a **pupa**.

A mosquito hatches out of the pupa.

MOTHS

Moths can be found all over the world and in many habitats. They usually fly at night and are often attracted to lights. Moths' bodies are often bigger and more furry than a butterfly's.

Unlike butterflies, most moths have feathery **antennae** and wings that are not very colorful.

antenna

head

abdomen

hind wing

How **BIG** is a **moth?**

12 inches

Smallest:
Sorrel pygmy moth

Largest:
Atlas moth

0.9 inches

forewing

Moths often lay their eggs on the underside of a leaf.

Moth Life Cycle

The female lays an egg.

A **larva** hatches out of the egg.

The larva grows into a **pupa**.

A moth comes out of the pupa.

PRAYING MANTISES

Praying mantises have large eyes that help them spot their **prey**. They eat other insects, such as beetles and butterflies.

A praying mantis whips out its spiky front legs to grab other insects. The spikes help it hold its wiggling prey while the mantis starts eating!

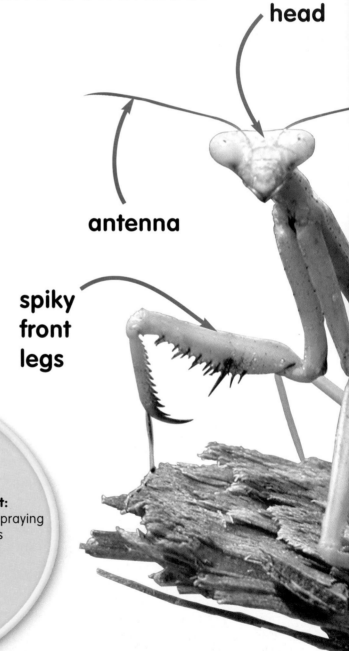

head

antenna

spiky front legs

How **BIG** is a **praying mantis?**

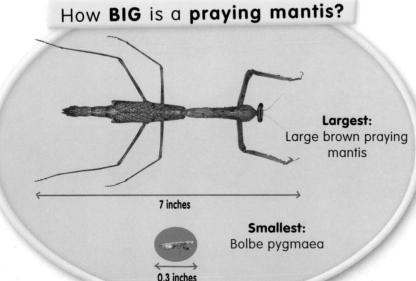

Largest:
Large brown praying mantis

7 inches

Smallest:
Bolbe pygmaea

0.3 inches

When a praying mantis is about to grab a meal, it holds its front legs up as if it were praying.

abdomen

Praying Mantis Life Cycle

The female mantis lays an egg. Mantis eggs are wrapped in a tissue-like covering.

A **nymph** hatches out of each egg.

The nymph develops into an adult mantis.

RAFT SPIDERS

Raft spiders are also known as fishing spiders. They stand on top of the water and grab insects, tadpoles, and even small fish.

A female raft spider spins a web like a tent, to hold her eggs. She guards them until they hatch.

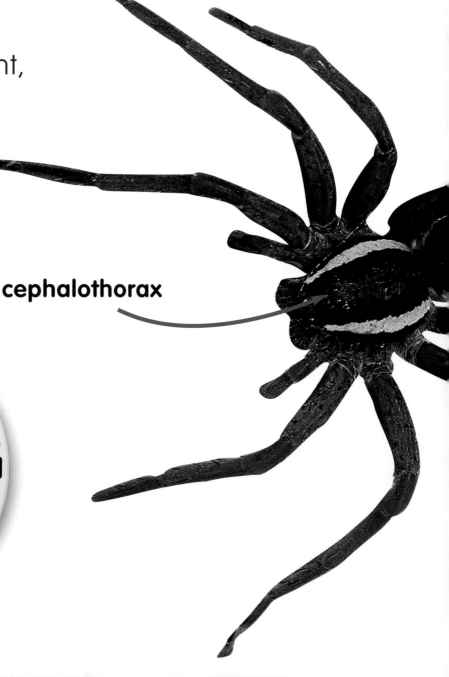

cephalothorax

REAL-LIFE SIZE
REAL-LIFE SIZE

Fen raft spider
1 inch

Hairs on the spider's legs help it feel slight movements in the water. This way, it knows if food is nearby!

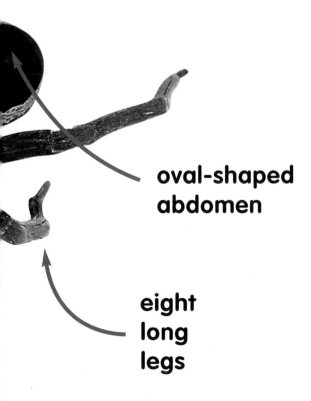

oval-shaped abdomen

eight long legs

Raft Spider Life Cycle

The female spider lays an egg.

A spiderling hatches from the egg.

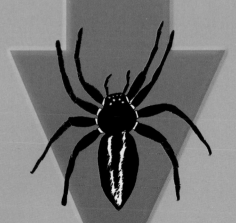

The spiderling becomes an adult.

69

RHINOCEROS BEETLES

Rhinoceros beetles have large horns, like a rhinoceros. They live in forests and use their horns to dig. Male beetles also use their horns to fight each other.

Rhinoceros beetles eat rotting fruit and **sap**.

three strong horns

spiky legs

How **BIG** is a **rhino beetle?**

Largest:
Megasoma
actaeon

Smallest:
Allomyrrhina
pfeifferi

4.7 inches

1.6 inches

Rhino beetles are very strong. They can carry loads up to 850 times their own weight.

very hard wing cases

Rhino Beetle Life Cycle

A female rhinoceros beetle lays an egg.

A **larva** hatches from the egg.

When full grown, the larva changes into a **pupa**.

A rhinoceros beetle hatches from the pupa.

SCORPIONS

Scorpions are related to spiders. They have eight legs, plus two strong claws for grabbing their **prey**. They eat insects and small animals.

Scorpions rest under rocks during the day and hunt at night. A female scorpion carries her babies on her back to keep them safe.

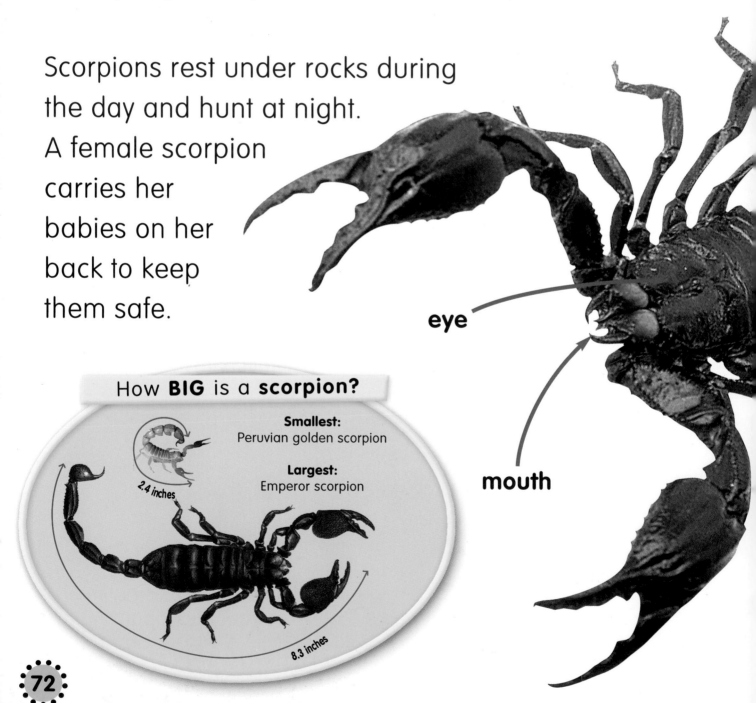

eye

mouth

How **BIG** is a **scorpion?**

Smallest:
Peruvian golden scorpion

Largest:
Emperor scorpion

2.4 inches

8.3 inches

A scorpion has a stinger at the tip of its tail. The sharp point sends deadly poison into the victim's body.

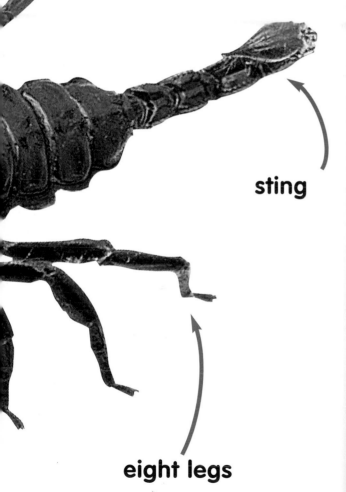

sting

eight legs

Scorpion Life Cycle

The female gives birth to a tiny, baby scorpion.

The young scorpion grows into an adult scorpion.

SLUGS

Slugs are part of an animal group called **mollusks**. Most mollusks live in or near water. Slugs live on land. They eat **fungi** and rotting plants.

A slug is like a snail without a shell. It moves by squeezing muscles on the underside of its body. It leaves a trail of slime wherever it goes!

body covered in slippery slime

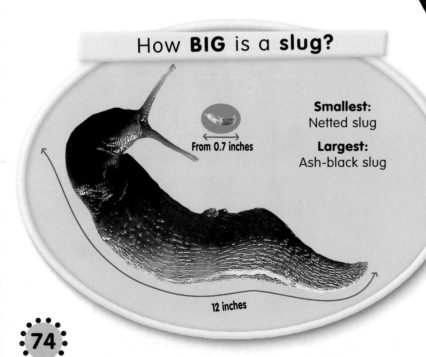

How **BIG** is a **slug?**

From 0.7 inches

Smallest:
Netted slug

Largest:
Ash-black slug

12 inches

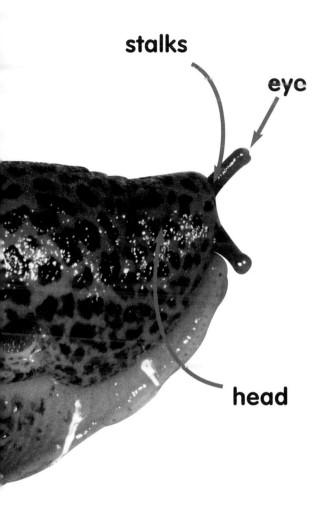

stalks

eye

head

Most slugs eat leaves, rotting fruit, and fungi. They are well known as pests because they eat the leaves of crops and garden plants.

Slug Life Cycle

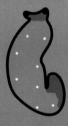

The female slug lays an egg.

A young slug hatches from the egg.

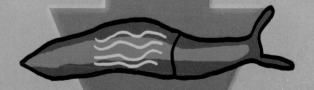

The young slug grows into an adult slug.

SNAILS

Snails are a lot like slugs, but they have hard shells. Snails that live on land eat plants. Some snails that live in ponds and oceans also eat live or dead animals.

A snail has a soft body that is protected by a hard shell. When the snail senses danger, it pulls its body inside the shell.

hard spiral shell

soft body

How **BIG** is a **land snail?**

Largest:
Giant African land snail

Smallest:
Ammonicera rota

0.04 inches

12 inches

eye

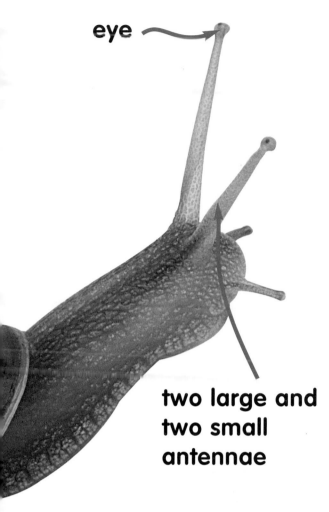

two large and two small antennae

In dry weather, a land snail can seal up the opening of its shell to keep from drying out.

Land Snail Life Cycle

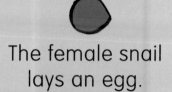

The female snail lays an egg.

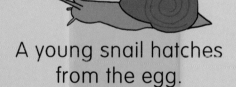

A young snail hatches from the egg.

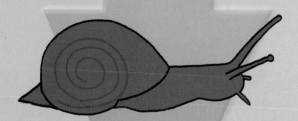

The young snail grows into an adult snail.

STAG BEETLES

Stag beetles live under logs and tree stumps. The **larvae** eat rotting wood and roots. The adults eat tree **sap**.

A male stag beetle has enormous jaws that look like a deer's antlers. He uses them to fight other males. Stag beetles also have wings.

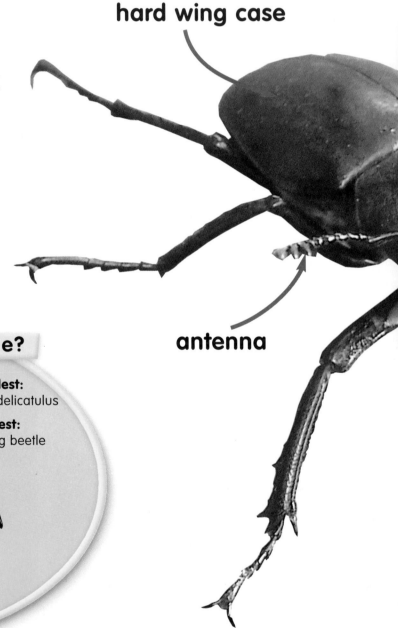

hard wing case

antenna

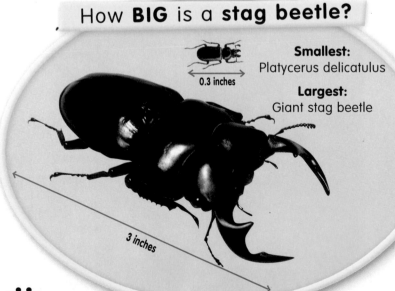

How **BIG** is a **stag beetle**?

0.3 inches

Smallest:
Platycerus delicatulus

Largest:
Giant stag beetle

3 inches

Male stag beetles are much bigger than the females.

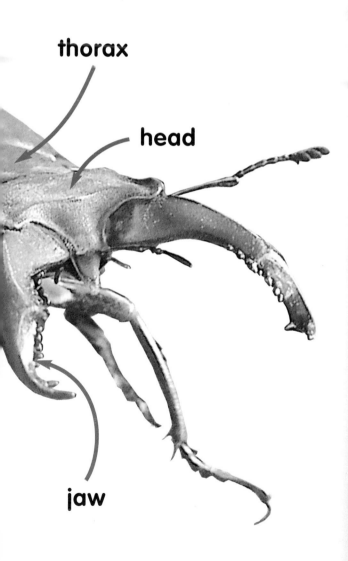

thorax

head

jaw

Stag Beetle Life Cycle

The female beetle lays an egg.

A **larva** hatches from the egg.

The larva grows and changes into a **pupa**.

The pupa grows into an adult stag beetle.

STICK INSECTS

There are about 2,000 kinds of stick insects. They use **camouflage** to hide from hungry birds. From the air, they look just like sticks! Stick insects wait until dark to move around and feed on leaves.

Some stick insects can make their own leg fall off if a **predator** grabs it. This gives the insect a chance to escape. The leg grows back later.

abdomen

six long, thin legs

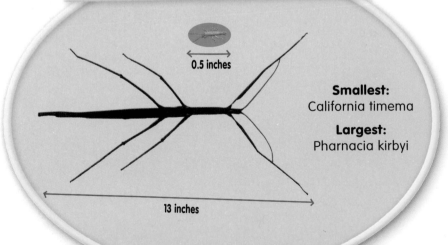

How **BIG** is a **stick insect?**

0.5 inches

Smallest:
California timema

Largest:
Pharnacia kirbyi

13 inches

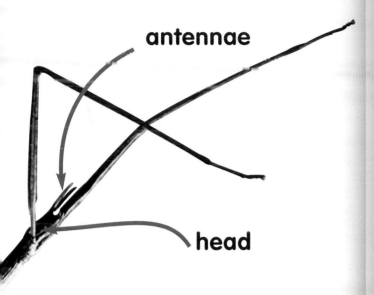

antennae

head

Some people keep stick insects as pets. If they are kept on thorny bushes they will grow spines to help camouflage themselves.

Stick Insect Life Cycle

The female stick insect lays an egg.

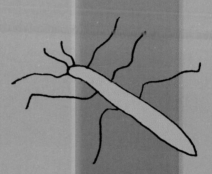

A **nymph** hatches from the egg.

The nymph grows into an adult stick insect.

STINK BUGS

Stink bugs are insects that are often found in farm fields. They feed on any crops they can find, such as grain and beans.

Stink bugs can give off an unpleasant smell when they are disturbed. They are also known as shieldbugs because of their shape.

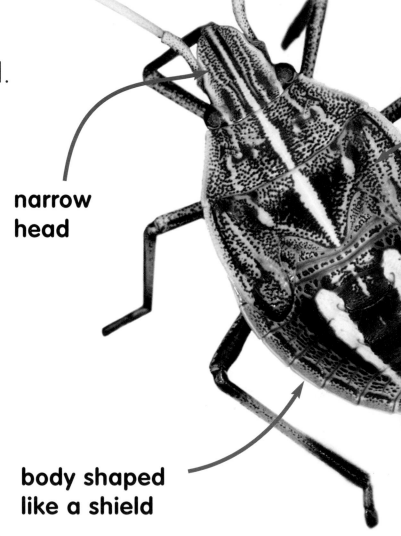

antenna

narrow head

body shaped like a shield

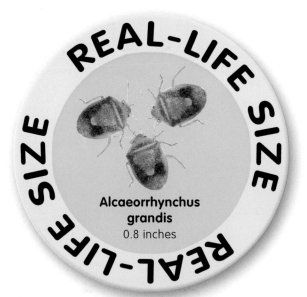

REAL-LIFE SIZE

Alcaeorrhynchus grandis
0.8 inches

The female bug lays her eggs on leaves. She guards the young **nymphs** when they hatch.

tough forewings that close over thin hind wings

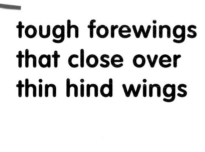

Stink Bug Life Cycle

The female stink bug lays an egg.

A **nymph** hatches from the egg.

The nymph grows up to be an adult stink bug.

TARANTULAS

Tarantulas are hairy spiders. Most are very large. They use sharp **fangs** to kill insects, lizards, frogs, small birds, and even snakes.

Tarantulas have a deadly bite that sends poison into their **prey**.

abdomen

strong jaws

one of two pedipalps, used to hold on to prey

How **BIG** is a **tarantula?**

0.2 inches

Smallest:
Spruce fir moss spider

Largest:
Goliath tarantula

11 inches

Tarantulas do not make a web. They hunt their prey on the ground.

eight hairy legs

Tarantula Life Cycle

The female tarantula lays an egg.

A spiderling hatches from the egg.

The spiderling grows into an adult tarantula.

TERMITES

Termites are insects that live in large **colonies**. The nests of some kinds of termites are tall towers of soil. Others are papery balls high up in trees. Termites eat plants and wood.

Termites have soft bodies and rounded **heads**. Only the king and queen have wings.

queen termite

workers

REAL-LIFE SIZE

Pacific dampwood termite
0.7 inches

Worker termites have no wings. They build the nest and take care of the young. Soldier termites have strong jaws. Their job is to protect the nest.

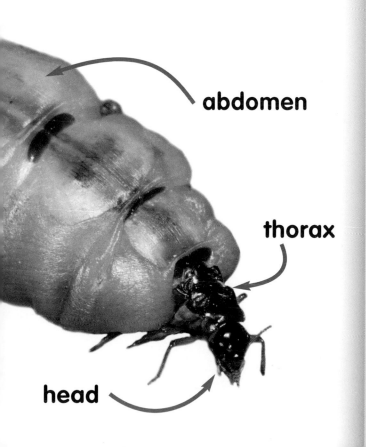

abdomen

thorax

head

Termite Life Cycle

The female termite lays an egg.

A **nymph** hatches from the egg.

The nymph grows into an adult termite. This is an adult soldier termite.

TREE NYMPHS

Tree nymphs are a type of butterfly. They are found mostly in rainforests. Like all butterflies, they sip liquid foods such as **nectar**.

The **forewings** of the tree nymph are almost twice as wide as they are tall.

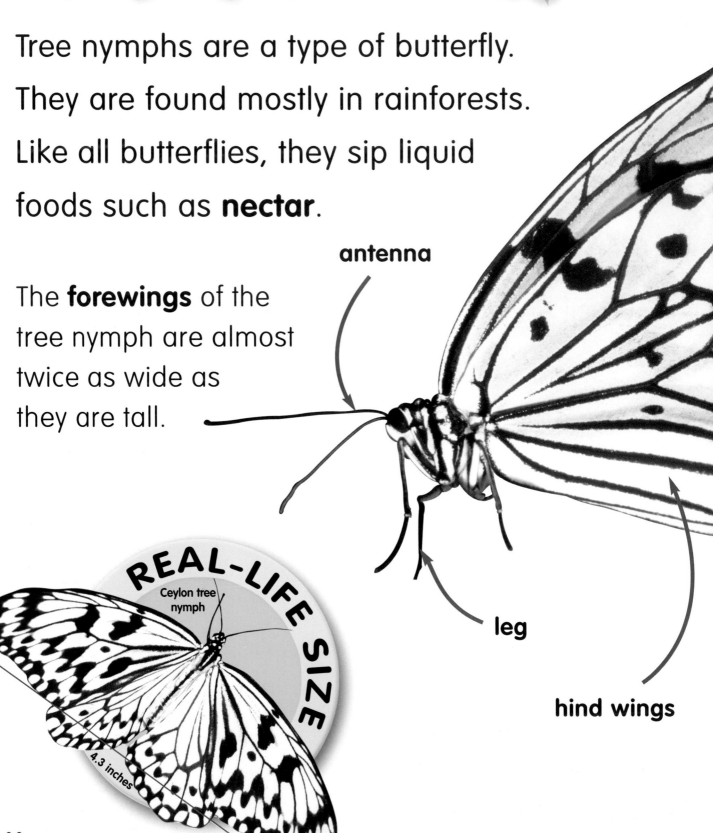

antenna

leg

hind wings

REAL-LIFE SIZE

Ceylon tree nymph

4.3 inches

wide forewings

Male tree nymphs give off a scent, or smell, that attracts females.

Tree Nymph Life Cycle

A female tree nymph butterfly lays an egg.

A caterpillar hatches from the egg.

When full grown, the caterpillar changes into a **pupa** or chrysalis.

A tree nymph butterfly hatches from the chrysalis.

WASPS

Wasps are a group of stinging insects. Some kinds live in **colonies**. Others live alone. Wasps like sweet foods such as fruit and **nectar**.

A worker wasp uses its stinger to **paralyze** caterpillars and other insects. They are used to feed the growing wasp **larvae**.

striped abdomen

transparent wings

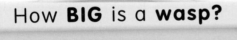

How **BIG** is a **wasp?**

0.005 inches

The picture is larger than real life so you can see it!

Smallest:
Dicopomorpha
echmepterygis

Largest:
Asian giant
hornet

1.8 inches

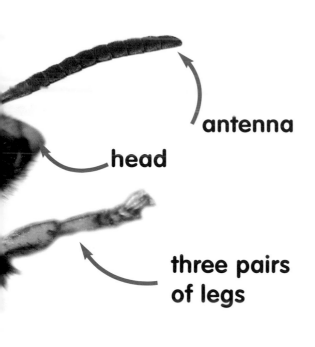

antenna

head

three pairs of legs

Some wasps can make paper by chewing on wood. They use the paper to build their nests. A finished nest may have thousands of cells (rooms).

Wasp Life Cycle

A female wasp lays an egg.

A **larva** hatches from the egg.

When full grown, the larva changes into a **pupa**.

A wasp hatches from the pupa.

WOLF SPIDERS

Wolf spiders hunt for their food and do not spin webs. They eat small animals and insects such as locusts and beetles. They usually hunt at night. Wolf spiders can see very well.

Wolf spiders have strong legs and can run very fast to catch their **prey**.

four large eyes and four small eyes

jaws

REAL-LIFE SIZE
REAL-LIFE SIZE

Carolina wolf spider
1.5 inches

These spiderlings will live on their mother's back until they are big enough to hunt on their own.

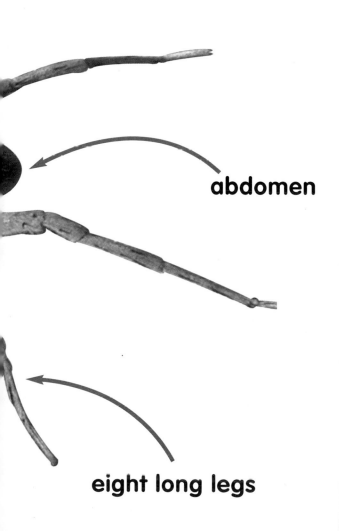

abdomen

eight long legs

Wolf Spider Life Cycle

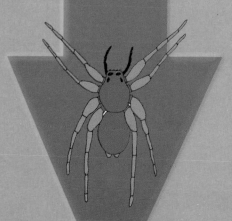

A female wolf spider lays an egg.

A spiderling hatches from the egg.

The spiderling grows into an adult wolf spider.

Glossary

abdomen: The last section of an insect's body.

antennae: Long, thin feelers on an insect's head that are used for tasting and touching.

burrow: To dig into the ground to hide or to live. Also an animal's home made by burrowing.

camouflage: When an animal's skin or fur color blends in with its background.

cerci: Spikes at the end of an insect's abdomen that sense movement. Just one spike is a cercus.

colonies: Groups of insects that live together and help each other survive.

compound eye: An eye with many surfaces that lets an insect see in many directions at one time.

evergreen: Any kind of tree that stays green and leafy in the winter.

fangs: Large, sharp teeth used for biting into prey.

forceps: The long claws of some bugs.

forewings: The front pair of wings, closest to the head.

fungi: Plantlike living things such as mushrooms and molds.

head: The front section of an insect, which contains the eyes, mouthparts, and antennae.

hibernate: To spend the winter in a deep sleep.

hind wings: The back pair of wings.

honeydew: A sweet liquid produced by aphids.

host: The animal on which a parasite (such as a flea) lives and feeds.

hover: To stay in one place in the air while flying.

invertebrates: Animals that have no backbone. Invertebrates include insects, worms, mollusks, spiders, and shellfish such as lobsters.

larva: The wormlike stage that some kinds of insects go through when they first hatch from an egg. A larva will change into a pupa before it becomes an adult. "Larvae" is the word for more than one larva.

mandibles: The biting mouthparts of some insects.

mollusks: A group of animals with soft bodies that includes snails, slugs, clams, and octopuses.

nectar: A sweet liquid made by flowers that attracts insects and some birds.

nymph: The young of certain kinds of insects. They hatch from an egg looking like a smaller version of their parents.

paralyze: To make an animal unable to move.

parasite: An animal that feeds on another animal without killing it.

pollen: Yellow dust that male flowers make to help them produce new seeds.

predator: An animal that eats other animals.

prey: An animal that is food for other animals.

pupa: The stage of some insects' lives between larva and adulthood. The insect goes through big changes while it is a pupa.

saliva: A liquid made by an animal's mouth or special glands (body parts).

sap: The liquid inside a tree or other plant.

sucker: A flat body part that allows an animal to cling to a surface.

thorax: The middle section of an insect's body, where the legs attach and where wings may attach.

transparent: Something that is see-through.

wing cases: The hard front wings of beetles that fold over and protect the back, flying wings.

Index

Picture credits

We would like to thank Ardea, Corbis, FLPA and Oxford Scientific Photo Library for the images used in this book.

Every effort has been made to trace the copyright holders and we apologize in advance for any unintentional omissions. We would be pleased to insert the appropriate acknowledgements in any subsequent edition of this publication.